Felix Domesticus

Mark Ellott

This is a book about cats and almost entirely nothing but cats. It's also got some cats in it – and then some more cats. If you like cats, you will probably like this book. If you don't like cats, you probably won't.

Mark Ellott Publishing

Copyright © Mark Ellott 2006

ISBN 1-4276-0292-1

All rights reserved. No part of this publication may be reproduced, stored in a retrieval system, or transmitted in any form or by any means, electronic, mechanical, photocopying, recording or otherwise, without the prior permission of the publishers.

All cats in this book are real and they take copyright infringement seriously.

For Frankie

…and the cats of course.

Felix Domesticus

In ancient Egypt, cats scavenged for food among the dwellings of people who lived along the banks of the Nile. There was good eating to be had in exchange for a little vermin control. There was even better eating to be had pretending to care about what the humans thought. A little responsive purr to a tickle behind the ear or a rub on the chin did no harm and if it made the people happy and they gave out free food, well, everyone stood to gain. And, if there's one thing cats understand completely, it is the principle of gain. "What's yours is mine" is their motto. Their other motto is "What's mine is mine, too."

The Ancient Egyptians thought they were getting a good deal; so much so, that they revered and even worshipped their feline companions. Now, that, for the cats, was the business. There was good eating to be had being a god. Getting sacrificed and mummified wasn't so cool, but it was one of the occupational hazards of being a living deity.

The wonderful thing about sharing your life with cats; it's a win-win situation. The ancient Egyptians thought they were getting the best of the bargain whereas the cats knew that *they* were.

Several millennia on, not much has changed.

Felix Domesticus, Calculating Cat

Tabby tiger, jellicle, ginger or calico;

Our green eyes follow you wherever you go.

From the street corner, on the shed roof;

We know where you've been, where you're going, where you're at;

Felix domesticus; the calculating cat.

***

Inscrutable and devious we watch all day;

We're not really asleep, don't hear what they say;

From the house window, the fence and the wall;

We know what you're doing, what you're thinking, where you're at;

Felix domesticus; the intelligence cat.

***

Cunning and wise, we daily take note;

Pretending not to notice as we groom our silken coat.

From the garden gate, the dark alleyway;

We know who you are, who you've seen, what you're at;

Felix domesticus; the enigmatic cat.

***

Feigning indifference we observe all around;

We'll pad along beside you with barely a sound;

From high in a tree, or across the road;

We know where you were, your plans today, what you're at;

Felix domesticus; the Delphian cat.

***

Green eyes, yellow eyes, golden and blue;

Eyes of every shade, hiding and watching you.

From the attic, the garage and under a car;

We keep tabs on where you go, who you see, what you're at;

Felix domesticus, the inquisitive cat.

***

Introduction

Welcome to Felix Domesticus; a series of diary entries by cats for cats. I'm Nefertiti, the matriarch of the group and I run things pretty much around here. As cats go, I'm of the more intelligent, though I do say so myself. Well, you have to be to keep ten other cats in order; and my, don't they need it. I'm forever chasing around just keeping the place together. I really don't know how people would manage without me. Well, they wouldn't and that's all there is to say on the matter. Modesty never got a cat anywhere, I always say. I'm also proof that intelligence and good looks are achievable in the same cool cat. Of course that upstart Caesar (more of him later) will have you believe otherwise.

As time goes on I'll introduce you to the rest of the tribe. Although, I really don't see why I should bother - after all, it's me you will want to know about. I am, after all, the boss - and don't you forget it.

Inscrutable Nef

I see Nef sitting on the chair;
On her face, that inscrutable stare;
"Where have you been? What will you do?
How would you cope if I don't keep a watch over you?"

***

I see Nef send my keys crashing to the floor;
Before looking around to see if there are any more.
"These things have to be done and if not my me;
They wouldn't get done at all, don't you see?"

***

I see Nef watching from the top of the drive;
Checking all's well as home I arrive.
"All those other cats would invade if I didn't take the time;
To keep a careful watch for what's yours and what's mine."

***

I see Nef soaking up the warm summer days;
Always alert with that impenetrable gaze.
"I need to know what going on around here;
For I am in charge, I do hope that's clear."

***

Caesar – The Urban Tiger

Caesar is one of our three tom cats. Now, Toms are darlings really and I wouldn't be without them, but they are rather useless about the house. There is a reason for this. Toms keep their brains in their balls and you know what happens to those…

So after six months, they become brainless dollops who lounge about the place contributing nothing but good looks. This brings me rather neatly to Caesar. Narcissism in a mackerel tabby coat is our Caesar. Of course, getting his picture displayed in the local camera shop didn't help matters.

He was about two years old when he posed for this picture and so taken by it was the local processing shop that they kept a copy for their display.

Did we hear the last of it? Did we indeed ever indeed! Ever since that picture he preens about asking "Am I looking good today?" Then giving us the answer… "I'm looking good…"

As decoration Caesar is perfect. As a contributor to the household his usefulness is limited, I can tell you. Ask him to catch a mouse or climb a tree and he wouldn't want to risk messing up his coat. Yet everyone loves him. Well, everyone except his sister, Bast and nieces, who will clip his ear and hiss at him just to put him in his place…

Sometimes I don't understand just what it is he does that annoys them so much. Apart, that is, from just walking into the room looking good.

***

"That Nefi isn't about is she? Eyes everywhere, that one. No - quick look, just in case - right. Now, it seems to me, that there's far too much about those queens for my liking. It's the Toms that are the top cats around here - and, I might add, the best looking. As the oldest Tom and the coolest thing on legs in the neighbourhood, there ought to be more about me. That's right, me, Caesar, fine specimen of tabby excellence that I am. Now, make sure you get my best side. I want my lionesque profile in shot.

Ahem, and just who has magnificent whiskers here? Hmm? Eh? Hey! I wasn't ready for that; I was just having a quick scratch before posing."

The Urban Tiger

I am the urban tiger with my tabby stripes;

My green eyes see all in the darkest of nights.

I am the urban tiger with my padded black paws;

I'll fight for my ground with tooth and claws.

I am the urban tiger, with my imposing profile;

I strut through the back gardens in regal style.

I am the urban tiger, beware my disapproving scowl;

With folded back ears, I'll face you off with a growl.

I am the urban tiger, the undisputed king;

Admire, all you mortals; did you see such a thing?

I am the urban tiger with my mackerel coat;

I'll deign to let you pet me with a purr in my throat.

I am the urban tiger, alert in repose;

As I lie by the radiator toasting my toes.

I am the urban tiger, good looking and serene,

The dandiest tom cat you'll ever have seen.

Thutmose – The Wanderer

Thutmose has several different names. Usually referred to as Thutmose grey toes - because he has a grey toe on each foot - he is also referred to by a number of less, shall we say, complimentary names, "miserable bugger" being the latest. Thutmose was a promising kitten for a tom - indeed; I had high hopes for him as he readily lent himself to such tasks as exploring the attic. I've included a picture - you can just about see me offering useful instruction.

Thutmose managed to avoid the dreaded snip for three years. The people who share our abode wanted him to father some kittens, so put off the inevitable until he had done his duty. Well, he did that alright. Ahmose now has two kittens and Berenike is the image of Thutmose - there's no guessing paternity with that one. Indeed, she is starting to show his attitude as well.

Anyway, I digress. Thutmose is a wanderer. Some tom cats are and that's all there is about it. It became the norm for him to disappear for a day or two at a time and the people got used to it and shrugged it off. "Oh," they would say, "That's just him being a tom cat." Then he disappeared for three weeks. That changed their tune, I can tell you. They were worried, we could tell. They would sit at their computers tapping in his details to lost cat searches and making telephone calls; all because the randy charlatan was off getting his end away with some tart down the road, no doubt. Then three and a half weeks later he wanders in bright and breezy and twice as ugly with that arrogant yowl of his, demanding dinner like nothing had happened.

***

That was the final straw for the humans - they whisked him down to the vets before you could say "Nefertiti is a very fine cat indeed" and he had the snip. Did that change him? Did it ever! He still wanders off and they still treat him like royalty when he deigns to honour them with his presence. The more aloof he is with them, the more they fawn for his attention. And they still say what a fine cat he is and what a delightful grey coat he has. I'm missing a trick here, I think.

Added to all of this, he now wants to establish himself at the top of the hierarchy. The effrontery! I am the top cat around here. He even had the nerve to chase me up the garden the other day. He chased ME! A quick boxing of his ears put paid to that little game, I can tell you. We'll be having none of that around here, thank you very much. Here's what the humans had to say:

"For just over three and a half weeks, Thutmose our grey and white tomcat went missing. As he usually disappears for several days at a time we were not too worried at first. Then as the days dragged by and one week became two weeks, we started to worry. We decided perhaps now was the time for action and set in motion the usual activities involved with missing pets; posters in the local Post Office and veterinary surgeons, contacting the pets search agencies, the local dogs and cats home, the RSPCA, and of course taking walks out where we know that he haunts. Near to the back of our house is a cycleway that runs through the common. This is cat heaven and I spent several trips walking and cycling in the area looking for him.

Then after nearly three and a half weeks he breezes in large as life, sits down and demands food. As if nothing had happened in the last three and a half weeks. It is only when the animal returns alive and well, that you start to realise just how worried you had become. I spent much of yesterday telephoning and e-mailing various agencies that we had contacted regarding his disappearance to let them know that he had turned up. Meanwhile, Thutmose is under house arrest while we arrange a trip to the veterinary surgeons for microchipping and of course the dreaded snip. Hopefully this will curb his wandering habits. And my, isn't it good to have him back."

***

As Thutmose had gone semi feral, the humans decided that some time as a house cat was in order. As I write this, he is power sleeping upstairs, which leaves one to wonder just what it is he gets up to when he disappears for days at a time over on the common. His daughters tried to make his acquaintance but were treated to the scowl and growl response. Not that they were fazed by this, Cleo has been warming them up for it with her hisses and scowls since they were born.

Mind you, the longer he stays in, the more of the old tarty Thutmose is revealed. Reluctantly, I have to admit that he's a fine cat with a friendly nature - for a Tom...

***

"Well, the humans have got me incarcerated, so I'll have to make the best of it. I'll try not to look as if I'm making the most of the "Nautically Nibblies" they are giving me. Hmm, this keyboard stuff isn't as difficult as that proper little Madam, Nefertiti makes out. I could make a go of this. Seeing as I'm confined, I might as well acquaint myself with all this computer stuff, such as

sitting on the scanner. That is what scanners are for, isn't it?

Mind you, it's been a long time since I got any window duty in... those other coves keep chasing me away so I have to wander about on the common. Let's see... hmm... raining today. Maybe I will stop indoors for a little longer.

Oh, yes, what's all this about two daughters? Nothing to do with me, guv, honest. You don't expect me to recall a brief encounter nearly six months ago, do you? It was all Ahmose's fault anyway, tarting about encouraging me, like... She should've taken precautions. I'm not admitting anything without a paternity test. CSA, you say? Nope, not me, guv. Thutmose? No that must be the other grey cat - three doors down, you can't miss him; his eyes are too close together; untrustworthy cove that one."

***

May 2005

That good for nothing layabout Thutmose was released from custody yesterday. The humans decided that he had been incarcerated enough and now was as good a time to see if he had amended his wayward ways.

Upon his release, he took Berenike for a walk around the local neighbourhood, and then he and his family spent the night playing tag and climbing trees. They came in this morning for breakfast before going out again. I can't help wondering how he would be after a long stretch.

So, did the humans' experiment work? Well, yes, it does rather look as if it has; for the moment. So we queens have to put up with another ragamuffin tomcat lurking about the place.

***

Some weeks later…

The humans are worried about Thutmose's wandering ways, still. Despite keeping him in, he continues to go off for two or three weeks at a time. Not that the rest of us worry; more room at the food bowls; but the humans seem to like him and want him around. Why? When they've got me? I don't understand. But, then, humans are a strange, irrational species and I'll never really comprehend them...

Anyway, they have come to the conclusion that the wandering Tut has a second home. They reached this conclusion because having disappeared for three weeks, he put on weight. So, they have decided that he isn't living rough when he wanders. Their cunning plan is to put a collar on him; despite them not liking collars on cats (none of us wear them). They are putting a tag on with their contact details in the hope that whoever is giving him succour will contact them. Of course, this could result in a tug of kitty exchange as the other home (if it exists) may decide that he is their cat and he is called Tiddles.

Still, they put the collar on last night; a purple one. And I must say, he does look rather dashing... I could almost fancy him myself.

***

After two weeks in the wilderness, Thutmose returned sans natty purple collar. There were no phone calls claiming that "Tiddles" was their grey cat. Nothing. So, as experiments go - this one was a complete and utter failure.

***

07/02/2006

Well, the humans' detective skills finally paid off. One of them went to post a letter yesterday and decided that as the wandering Tut hadn't been by for a couple of weeks to try calling him from the back of the gardens. Our garden backs onto other gardens and they can be accessed by going to the other side of the cul-de-sac. Sure enough, Thutmose responded to the call. Like a guilty child caught out, he was all affectionate. The hideaway has now been narrowed down to the garage directly opposite our garden - the missing windows provide easy access and it is a nice little place for a cat to hide. The resident cat is usually indoors, so it is a matter of stealing its food when it isn't looking. So, the runaway Tut wasn't so far away after all.

***

12/05/2006

Thutmose's second home was finally uncovered today. As we suspected, he was only a short distance from his first home. Nicknamed "Bandit" for his tendency to steal the home cat's food, he has been made welcome, which is why he stays. He has a lovely nature, they tell us. Well, we know that, already. I just wish he would come home more often.

Free is the spirit

Free is the untamed spirit that lives within me;

I am the wild wraith that will always be free.

Love me if you will, but tomorrow I'll be gone.

Know that I'm here for a moment;

Then I'll move on;

Gravelled is the road that I travel along.

The sun and stars will be my guide;

The wind in my fur pushes me onward once more.

I need no one at my side;

As I seek somewhere to explore.

I slink beneath the hedgerows on a moonlight night;

And skulk through fields in my endless flight.

Free is the untamed spirit that lives within me;

I am the wild wraith that will always be free.

Love me if you will, but tomorrow I'll be gone.

Know that I'm here for a moment;

Then I'll move on;

Gravelled is the road that I travel along.

Alone with the eagles' call in mountains high;

Drawn to the shores of the unrelenting sea;

Love me if you must, but know that loving me;

Means I'll be gone before dawn, gone with a sigh.

Free is the untamed spirit that will always be me;

I am the wild wraith that will always be free.

Love me if you will, but tomorrow I'll be gone.

Know that I'm here for a moment;

Then I'll move on;

Gravelled is the road that I travel along.

***

Ptolemy

Ptolemy looks much like his mother - a tabby striped tiger with a white tip on his tail. The humans tend to use terms like "not the sharpest tool in the box" although I'm not too sure what they mean by this. His claws are very sharp. Ptolemy is typical of a tom cat, though; not very bright, yet generous in nature.

Sometimes he will catch a mouse - more often he will steal it from one of his sisters. Once he brought one into the house much to the annoyance of the humans who chased it around the room until it shot down a hole in the skirting and disappeared. Ptolemy kept watch on the hole for a while in the hope that the mouse would reappear. More likely it went under the floor and outside through a ventilation brick. He still harbours a hope that it will return and from time to time will look at the hole to see if there are any developments. None yet, of course, and the brighter cats in the tribe realise this.

Most of us give him short shrift - particularly when he tries to assert himself as top cat. I've been known to box his ears on occasions for that offence. His usual trick is to slink up to his victim and lick their ears. Very nice, we all like the occasional ear lick.... mmmmmmmm. Then the blighter bites it. This results in a hiss, spat and flying fur with Ptolemy crashing through the cat flap with his offended victim in hot pursuit.

Since Ahmose arrived in the summer of 2004, Ptolemy has a comrade in arms. He mothers her and she returns the affection. Oh, well, that saves my ears being bitten, I suppose. Since she had the kittens, he nannies them, too and she doesn't mind. So all too often there is a thundering of feet, rattling of the cat flap and the humans look at each other and say "Mungojerrie and Rumpelteazer and that's all there is to say about that".

This picture is typical of him - looking as if butter wouldn't melt. Don't you believe it. He is doubtless plotting some nefarious crime against another cat.

Ptolemy Tom

Ptolemy tom looks like his mum;

But there the similarity ends.

He'll jump and he'll tease;

Bites other cats' ears if you please;

It drives them all round the bend.

So when there's a bicker and a spat;

A quick hiss and a splat;

They will always say;

"It's Ptolemy tom in the middle of the fray."

   ***

Ptolemy tom looks like his mum;

But there the similarity ends.

He'll wind up the others;

Sisters, uncle and mother,

Till it drives them round the bend.

So when there's a snarl and a scrap,

A crash through the catflap;

Someone will say;

"It'll be Ptolemy tom in the middle of the fray."

   ***

Ptolemy tom looks like his mum;

But there the similarity ends.

Always good for the game;

To the others it's a pain,

But to the kittens he's a friend;

So when a stampede sweeps through the house;

Or someone's chasing a mouse;

The answer they'll say;

Is "Ptolemy tom's in the middle of the fray."

   ***

Hamlet, the Cat Who Came In From the Cold

When we lost our first Cleo in an accident in the late summer of 1997, we were devastated. At three years old she was just coming into her prime and that the accident was ultimately our fault made the loss harder to bear. Then Tiffany succumbed to a melanoma on New Year's Day 1998. We decided that Bast, then approaching six months should have a litter of kittens to compensate for the gap left by these two cats. The decision being that we would keep two of the litter and find homes for any surplus (we kept them all as it turned out).

During the early spring of 1998, Bast came on heat for the first time and went calling. Several toms appeared about that time, but one proved persistent and saw the others off on short order, a large ginger bruiser with a limp and a gammy eye.

When the kittens were born, one was a pure tortoiseshell with a slightly Persian face; two were tabbies with red stripes while the tom, Ptolemy, was the image of his mother. Hatshepsut, Cleo junior and Isis gave away their father's genes – the ginger bruiser. Indeed, Cleo looked just like him and shared the same scowl.

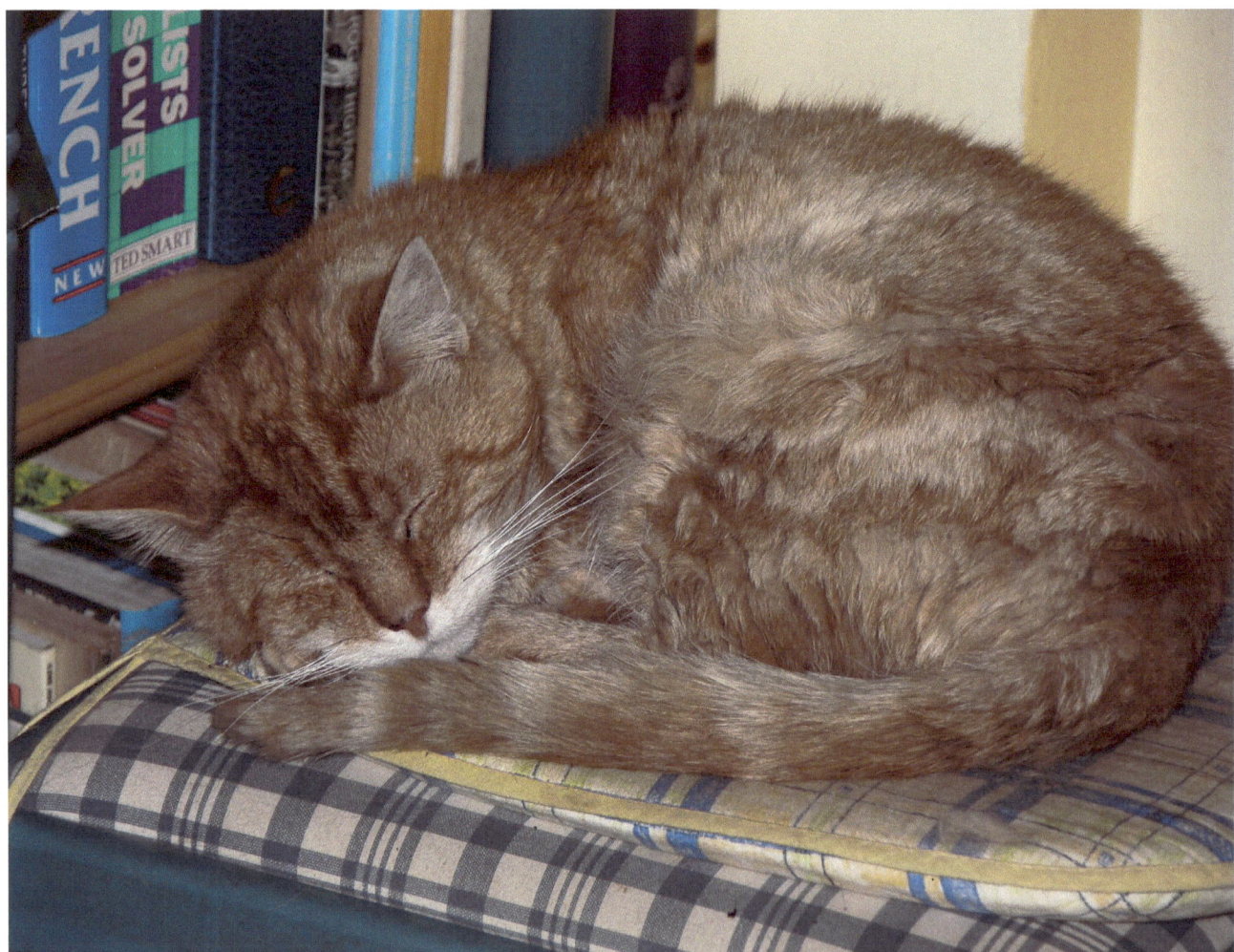

The father stayed. Sometimes he would be seen sneaking into the kitchen and scurry out if he detected us watching. Clearly a feral cat who spent his life scrounging what he could before being chased away he expected the same from us. Over then next few years he realised that we didn't chase him away and all too frequently he would be found making himself at home either in the front room or in the dining room on "his" chair.

We called him Hamlet after the picture Frankie's brother bought us that hangs in the kitchen. Depicting a rather more elegant cat than this one, its pale ginger coat was similar enough for the name to stick.

As the years passed, Hamlet became ever bolder. He still didn't like to be touched although when eating would tolerate a gentle head stroke. Winters were spent indoors and summers were spent out patrolling the territory, returning for food and sleep.

We became used to him being around. Never exactly our cat – and never getting too close, we were as near to home as he had known and he was as near to a pet as he was ever likely to get.

We knew that he had suffered the rigours of living a feral life, but resisted taking him to the vet as not only would he be difficult to capture, doing so would be traumatic for him. So as long as the stiff leg and cloudy eye didn't appear to trouble him, we left him to it.

Late in 2002, he started to deteriorate. First he stopped grooming. Frankie persevered with combing him to the accompaniment of hisses of rage before he decided that enough was enough and he scuttled out of the cat flap in disgust. This didn't stop him returning a short while later to take up his place on the favourite chair, though.

Then he started to lose weight. When he stopped eating, we decided that trauma or not, he needed to see a vet.

The prognosis was much as expected. He was an old cat – probably ten years or more. He had lost some teeth and those he had were scaled. He had a heart murmur and his kidneys were diseased. We had three choices; hospitalise while he was re-hydrated, with the chance that he would live a few days longer, have him put down, or palliative care while letting nature take its course.

The torment of a trip to the vets was bad enough.

Another, for whatever reason was more than we felt that he should have to suffer. Hamlet's time was here. We decided that he should be allowed the dignity of dying in familiar surroundings where we could make him as comfortable as possible. Frankie commented that he had decided to give up – he'd had enough. Two days later, he slipped away in his sleep, almost exactly five years after he had breezed into our lives.

We never knew where he came from or how old he was, exactly. He lived by taking what he needed to survive while spreading his genes as far as he could. The evidence of that is the suspiciously high ginger content found in the tiger stripes on tabby cats around here. He neither wanted nor needed our affection. He gave us four beautiful cats – nothing more. Yet he leaves a gap that he never intended to fill.

As Samuel Johnson would have said, here lived a very fine cat indeed. A free spirit who kept his dignity to the end, Hamlet was a true cat.

Penfold Does a Captain Oates

10th November 2004

Our old ginger cat, Penfold departed this world sometime between last night and this morning. I think he suffered a stroke last week and was certainly blind. Despite this he tried to carry on as best he could; taking a daily constitutional down our garden, through next door, up to the front and back into ours. Yesterday was different. After twenty minutes or so, he had not reappeared, so I set about looking. He was nowhere to be found. For a cat that doesn't go far, this was ominous. I just had a feeling. This morning, I found him curled up at the bottom of the garden and buried him under his favourite sunning spot.

In the grand scheme of things, the death of a seventeen year old cat who had a good long life isn't much - but he was our cat and we will miss him.

A Sonnet for Penfold

My friend we part after so short a time;
Your company was a bright light briefly shone;
Oh, but your life was much shorter than mine;
Today all but your memory is gone.
***

I value what we had though it is long past;
I gaze at those pictures of the sun on your fur;
My, did our time travel by so fast;
No longer will I hear the sound of your purr.
***

Laden with snow is the grey winter sky;
As I long for the warm days of spring;
Quietly, I visit the spot where you now lie;
After you, I can think of only one thing.
***

You see, I knew it, I've been smitten;
By the tiny mews of a springtime kitten.
***

Isaac Newton and the Catflap

Let me tell you about my experiments for determining the physical nature of the universe. Of course the humans will have you believe that one of their ancestors Isaac Newton did all of this years ago. Well, what they don't tell you is that he had a cat. Who do you think knocked things off for him to watch them fall? Well it wasn't magic, was it? How do you think the apple fell? It didn't shake itself out of the tree. Cats discovered the existence of gravity. And if it wasn't for his cat, he would never have managed to work out the spectrum of light - we did that, too. That is why Isaac Newton made the first catflap - with guidance, of course - to enable his cat to move freely about the experimentation area and give direction as necessary. Someone had to show him how to position his prisms.

Ahem... getting a bit carried away there.... I'll come back to the catflap in a minute.

Now, if you want to check out my experiments, this is how you do it. Get up onto a suitable surface. Don't worry if the humans tell you not to, this makes it all the more interesting. Now, find a suitable object. Something that will make a lot of noise when it lands will be ideal. A tiled floor below is even better. I particularly like keys and spectacles as they make a nice jingly sound. Now, extend one claw and carefully hook it under the object. Look around you to make sure that there is an audience and purposefully drag the object with your claw to the edge of the surface and watch it drop. This should elicit gasps of admiration from the humans (or did they say it was exasperation?) accompanied by a satisfying noise on landing.

You have just proved that gravity exists. Feel free to practice this at home.

Anyway, back to the catflap. While Isaac Newton is accredited with discovering gravity and the nature of the universe, this just isn't true. He is also credited with his laws about the nature of forces and such stuff. This doesn't bother me too much. I just continue to test gravity every so often to check that it works and think no more of it. I mean, providing there's food on the plate, water in the pond and somewhere to bask what more could a self-satisfied cat want? Oh, yes, the freedom to come and go as one pleases. That was Newton's greatest achievement; far greater than all that physics stuff; the catflap. Apparently he was far too busy messing about with prisms and things, trying to discover the nature of light to be bothered with letting his cat in and out, which is a bit annoying if you ask me. We cats are always on the wrong side of the door - *that* is the nature of the universe. The catflap neatly solves the problem of lazy people who cannot be bothered to let us in and out at our whim. We can do it ourselves. The kittens didn't take long to figure that one out...

The Biscuit

Hatshepsut is a cat with airs - well, aren't we all? She is a cat who has ideas above her station in life (which is below me). Don't they all, indeed? Hatshepsut - of Hamlet and Bast, is a cat with many names. Hatshepsut became Hattie, then Hat. Then, as the humans are inclined, it grew longer again. It became Hat, the cat. As this rhymed with the nickname of a notorious gangster murdered by the Kray gang in the sixties (Jack the Hat McVitie), she became Hat the cat McVitie. McVities make biscuits... hence the moniker, "The Biscuit". Warped, I know, but it is a cross we cats have learned to bear - it sort of compensates when you consider free food for life.

Hat is a cat with eyes that bore into you. A stare from those peepers will freeze even the most determined kitten. They may try to take her place on the duvet, but they try in vain. So, too does her mother, Bast, who will defer to her wayward daughter on such matters - well, usually after a hiss and spat exchange. She will bounce onto the duvet, take up her place between the people and turn around three times before settling down. "It's my place, darling, and don't you forget it." Even I tend to let her have that one - the agro is never worth it...

And then there's the matter of climbing trees. Very arboreal is our Hattie. With her orange tabby coat she blends in nicely, which is useful for watching what the humans get up to without being observed herself. Well, it would be if she didn't get stuck and wail to be helped down. Some cats just can't cut it.

Hattie up a Tree

Hattie up a tree;
Queen of all she can see.
"With my tabby camouflage, I can see you;
But you can't see me."
      ***

How did she get there?
Now she's stuck in her leafy lair.
She'll try to pretend it's all just fine;
And put on a nonchalant air.
      ***

Hattie might fall down;
She doesn't like being the clown.
She holds onto her fragile dignity
With a disapproving frown.
      ***

Hattie up a tree;
Surveying all there is to see.
"With my tabby camouflage, this is my place;
Just look up at me."
      ***

Softly a gentle breeze;
Rustles through the leaves;
Her paws are unsteady on her chosen branch;
"Can I come down now, please?"
      ***

The Wittering Cat

Isis is much like T.S. Eliot's Rum Tum Tugger. Contrary and curious she is not like the other cats. One of Bast's kittens, she inherited her father's ginger genes and these show through her tabby coat.

This cat neither ventures upstairs nor outside the humans' boundary fence. Indeed, the garden is her territory and other cats venture in at their peril. She will wait on the shed roof and survey her domain. If the humans enter the garden she will rush up to them and squawk loudly at them. Indeed, she will follow them and witter, chirruping and squeaking as if she wants something, but no one has worked out what it is, yet. Weird. We usually just leave her alone. Indoors she will settle in her basket under the chair and woe betide any cat who dares to usurp that place.

Like her brother Ptolemy, she will take interest in the wildlife. Well, mice and voles. Unlike Ptolemy, she is more than happy to beat the living daylights out of fake mice. She has a grey stuffed mouse that she guards jealously and regularly beats into submission. Once, it had fur... Also, like Ptolemy she will occasionally inspect a hole in the skirting because a mouse once hid there and you never know, one day it might just come out again.

Bast

Bast is the mother of four of our extended family. She is also a cat with a serious attitude. This, I suppose, is why her three daughters also have a bad attitude. Bast (aka Baz) will spend most of her day sitting on things. Laps are the preferred option if she can secure one. Indeed, when the ape-people are wanting to use their computers, Baz will rush ahead of them, bounding gracelessly up the stairs to the computer room, leap (flollup) onto the side (which is an achievement given her lack of aerodynamic shape, I can tell you) and tramples across the keyboard - whereupon the ape-person will lift her bodily onto his or her lap. Mission accomplished.

Her attitude to other cats is one of "this is my place" and enter it at your peril. Those who do will be swiftly boxed on the ears and greeted with a loud hiss. If it's Caesar, then an extra loud, long hiss is in order and possibly a hefty clout with claws extended - and he's her brother.

She has a penchant for the bed. This can be a problem - so too do I and I am the boss. Baz sometimes forgets this little nicety and dares to hiss in my direction. I give her short shrift, I can tell you. I don't take any nonsense from little tabby cats with a big attitude, you just see if I don't!

I always think this picture makes her look like a little Buddha. Don't be fooled, this cookie is dozing with her eyes open. The snoring tends to give things away.

Bast has always been a tubby cat. Following her litter of kittens, she never quite got her figure back. A cat will always grow whiskers that allow it to get through gaps. The whiskers will grow to the width of the cat. Bast's are magnificent. Hence the moniker she has gained...The magnificent whisker. Indeed, she is.

Fathers and Daughters

Hamlet was the original Growltiger. Ginger coated with one good eye, a torn ear, limp and bad attitude he appeared on our territory when Bast was on heat. He sired four kittens and didn't realise that his job was now done and that he should do the honourable thing and vacate the premises. He stayed - pinching our food and ingratiating himself with the humans. The more he snarled and hissed at them, the more they tried to appeal to his better nature. Hah! Better nature indeed. He didn't have one. We all kept our distance. He liked to think that he was top cat around here, but that was just us letting him think that.

Take a good long look at that cat. Once, I guess, he was a good looking tom. By the time we knew him, the years had been rough and he was a bad attitude on legs and threadbare at the seams. His daughter, Cleo picked up where he left off when he died in 2003. Take a look at this picture and see the family resemblance:

The same set of the head, the same broad face and dammit! The same bad attitude. When Berenike and Arsinoe were born, the rest of us tended to be tolerant - well, they are only kittens and they don't realise that other cats' tails are not toys. A quick boxing of the ears usually gets the message across - temporarily, at least. Cleo will adopt a different approach. She will walk into the room and survey it for low flying kittens. If they are detected, she will hiss loudly in

their general direction before taking up residence and settling down to sleep. Woe betide any kitten that dares to ignore that warning. A quick trip to next Wednesday week is in store for those that do.

Curiously, she is friendly to the humans who seem to appreciate cats with a bad attitude. I really must take note of this and try it sometime.

***

And while we are on the subject of fathers and daughters; Berenike is still her daddy's girl, even if Daddy isn't so sure.

French Connections

Summer 2005

The humans are away at the moment. They think I don't know where they are. However, I am well aware of their whereabouts in southern France. Indeed, I know the exact location. This is due to the Feline Bureau of Intelligence. This is a worldwide intelligence gathering organisation dedicated to the eventual feline domination of the world by stealth - and free cat food for life. The FBI is not to be confused with that other organisation; the Canine Intelligence Agency - which isn't. They spend rather more time sniffing bums than is entirely healthy for my liking as well as running round in circles and slobbering over people. Such activities get in the way of effective intelligence gathering. Anyway, come the revolution, all dogs will be enslaved to do our bidding - as is only proper...

Oh, sorry, getting a bit carried away there. The FBI has a French connection and our agent in southern France is a calico cat codenamed Honey (Miel). Unbeknown to the humans who think she is just being friendly when she goes into their house and scrounges milk, she is gathering vital information on their activities and feeding it back to the spymaster general - that's me, in case you hadn't worked it out.

So, we know exactly where they are and there is no escape. The French Connection is keeping us well informed.

***

The humans have returned. The cheeky blighters expect us to behave as if nothing has happened, like we weren't abandoned for two weeks. Hah! Well, I did elicit a tickle behind the ear and Berenike did nuzzle their faces. When she nipped their noses they complained though.

I'm pleased to announce that our French Connection is busy training up the next generation of recruits:

Summer 2006

The humans are in France again. I wonder if they get the feeling that they are being watched?

Ahmose

Ahmose joined the tribe in the summer of 2004. A very strange looking kitten she was, indeed. All harlequin markings, ungainly legs and a squiffy left eye. As she grew, the slimmed down and her proportions became more elegant. Until she had her kittens. Since then, she has put on a comfortable fluffy paunch. While being an odd looking cat, she is, without doubt one of the most friendly – it's the ginger genes. Ginger cats tend to be tarts and Ahmose is no exception.

From my perspective, I'm more than pleased with her education. As you know, I've been training kittens for the last ten years. One of my training grounds is the attic. Exploring the attic is an important feline activity. After all, you never know what people will put up there if not properly supervised and audited. Bast was a promising kitten, but she just tends to find a warm spot and doze off. Thutmose was an excellent learner but seems to have lapsed in favour of the gardens opposite. So, I'm left with Ahmose - an inquisitive cat who has lived up to the early promise shown in kittenhood. I'm hoping that Berenike will follow in her mother's excellent pawsteps. She and her sister took to shinning up trees like born naturals and show all the signs of following in Ahmose's pawsteps.

Oh, and Ahmose does like her boxes…

Cats are not dogs. Dogs are rufty-tufty knockabout oafs. They're friendly enough but far too familiar. They also lack dignity. I dread to think what they roll around in; I just know it smells like something died. Cats on the other hand understand deportment. We cats are dignified creatures. We look upon canine brutes with considered disdain - as they deserve. You won't find cats doing anything undignified...

I said; cats are dignified creatures… Oh, never mind…

Boxes

Some of you may recall the human childrens' book "My Cat Likes to Hide in Boxes". Of course, this is true of all cats. Put a box in the room and we will happily oblige by claiming it. Boxes are very useful; they provide a convenient vantage point and that all important impromptu bed. Every self respecting cat knows what a box is for...

Some cats are more incorrigible than others. Ahmose doesn't worry whether the box is too small; she just stretches it to make it fit. Berenike follows in her mother's pawsteps. That family will always let the side down. No dignity, you see; none at all. I despair, I really do.

The Box

This is my box and don't you forget it;
My box is all cosy and dark therein.
This is my box even if it doesn't quite fit;
I'll just stretch it out until I can get in.
      ***

This is my box, my new hideaway;
Where the others can't see me looking at them.
This is where I'll be resting, stopping all day;
What are these kittens doing here, then?
      ***

These kittens they have no respect, don't you see?
To them if it's empty it's theirs all the same.
This is my box and it just isn't free.
They take what they want; it's all just a game.
      ***

This is my box; that I claimed for my lair.
Now the kittens have taken it, and it just isn't fair.
      ***

Kittens

25th May 2005 18:00

As I write this, Ahmose is pausing between kittens. She has two healthy kittens. Unfortunately, the third (the firstborn) was stillborn after a protracted labour. The veterinary surgeon said that this was due to its size and this being Ahmose's first pregnancy. Still can't help wondering if we could have done something, though. I probably always will.

Looks like it could be a long night.

22:00

Looks like that's the lot. A litter of three with two survivors. We were planning to keep one anyway. So what's another one?

Hello to Berenike and Arsinoe

Arsinoe

Berenike

June 2005

T.S. Eliot tells us that kittens these days are just not trained. Well, in the Nefertiti Academy for Wayward Kittens, they certainly are. Graduates can climb trees, catch all sorts of woodland animals, keep inventories of the cupboards and carry out scientific experiments to prove the existence of gravity using keys, spectacles and ornaments (failing that, anything that comes within claw reach will do).

I've been watching the development of Ahmose's kittens very closely these past five weeks. This is an important matter. As the matriarch, their education is of prime concern to me. That they are both queens is a good sign. I don't usually waste effort trying to educate the toms - they make poor micecatcher generals and their investigative instincts are non-existent. As for tree climbing, oh, please, spare me...

Now, of the two kittens, Arsinoe (the calico kitten) is perhaps the least equipped for the tasks I have in mind. She is a dear, but somewhat slow. Berenike (the black and white kitten) is the one already showing good investigative instincts - just like her mother, she will be an excellent learner. She has already grasped the significance of keys. Excellent, excellent. This kitten will go places, just you wait and see. Of course, if their mother wasn't so possessive, matters would be simpler...

July 2005

Ahmose's kittens had their first taste of the great outdoors today. Ahmose fussed about like, well, like a mother, herding and chirruping as she does. She really must get used to the idea that at six and a half weeks old, they are growing up and don't need her to fuss so much. But fuss, she does. Her own mother was like it.

***

Kittens grow up so quickly. Within six months, Berenike and Arsinoe were small cats as evidenced by the portraits that follow.

On Being Cute Kitties

Part of the arrangement between people and cats is the "cute kitty". Cats are, of course, anything but cute. We are wild hunters with sharp teeth and claws. Evil killers that lurk in the suburban undergrowth, we dare all who come our way to take their chance. Yet, despite the evidence, people expect us to be cute. If we want to keep the gravy train running, it's a part we have to play – and, my, don't we play it well? A box or a piece of string is all we need for this illusion to work effectively. A piece of string never loses its appeal. Arsinoe manages to maintain possession of her box while watching a piece of string. And, if we can get the people to do the work for us all the better. If they ever find out, there will be trouble, though, so don't tell 'em.

Just what is the attraction of bookshelves? Strange, dusty old things, books. People like them, but cats? No accounting for taste, I suppose… This getting up onto shelves and such is becoming a habit. I know Hattie does it and now Ahmose has started. Then, blow me down; Arsinoe is scrabbling about in the bookshelf. These kittens today, I just don't know…

A little bit of string
Is a fascinating thing.
I can't resist a little bat.
Take that and that and that!
    ***

A little bit of string,
A dangly wriggly thing.
I'll give it a jolly fine splat
It won't escape this little cat!
    ***

Saturday morning sorting out is always smoother when a cat lends a hand to help out. Berenike is more than willing to oblige. There was a drawer in here a moment ago, I wonder where it went? Better take a look and see if I can find it…

The boxes still appeal. Indeed, if you want to catch a cat, just put out a box. There's no need to use bait, the box is the bait. I suppose there is no chance now that Ahmose will ever learn decorum or elegance. Mind you, Bast isn't much better…

Chess

Terry Pratchett gave the game away with his book The Unadulterated Cat - illustrated by Gray Jolliffe. Cat chess has been around for a long time, certainly since the time of the ancient Egyptians, and Mr Pratchett let the cat out of the bag…

The rules are simple; every cat in a neighbourhood must observe as many other cats as possible without being observed themselves. Therefore a good vantage point is necessary. Also, it is possible to play in teams, so I have 11 pairs of eyes at my disposal and we can work shifts. After all, a game can go on for months or even years at a time. A rotational shift system gives us the edge. Well, it would if Bast didn't fall asleep at her post.

The playing board is as large or small as is necessary. It may be a couple of back yards, a whole neighbourhood or small town. It changes dynamically depending on the game. Pratchett pondered on the possibility of a higher mystical level to the game. Of course there's a higher mystical level, but you don't think we'd share it with you lot, do you?

My preferred vantage point is at the top of the drive. It may not be very high, like the upstairs window, but it does give me a good view down the road and I have to keep a beady eye on that black cat three doors down opposite. Oh, and there's that ginger cat, Fudge who needs supervision. He seems to think he's one of us…

Naturally, the most powerful piece on the board is the Queen. Which is right and proper, as things should be. And, being the older queen that means I am the most powerful player on this board. So just mind your Ps and Qs.

***

The window is always a good vantage point and we use it regularly. Even Bast gets some window duty in occasionally. Well, that's when she isn't asleep at her post. This is usually detected by the gentle snoring emanating from the direction of the window blinds. She thinks we haven't sussed it…

Painting and decorating means that the humans take down the window blinds. This is a mixed blessing as the workload involved is doubled I have to watch what they are doing as well as keeping an eye on outside events. The humans did some painting and decorating over the Easter weekend. Naturally, I was called in to carry out the supervision.

I think that wall needs a second coat, there… Yes, just there, I can see a bit of the previous coat showing through. That's the problem with this painting and decorating business; with the blinds down, I don't know whether I should be concentrating on the inside and checking the quality of the work, or watching outside… I know, what about both?

Oy, whose car is that pulling up outside?

Besides, Berenike is always willing to help out, so that's the workload halved.

Ptolemy, meanwhile, hasn't figured out what type of window we mean:

Summer

Summer; that season when the air is redolent with the heady scent of flowers; the borders resplendent with the colour of geraniums, delphiniums, Canterbury bells and clematis. Summer; languid, mellow and indolent; a time for watching the world pass by under hazy blue skies, with fluffy white clouds and vapour trials. Summer is a time to reflect, while doing nothing in particular; a time for just being. Summer; the sound of far off lawn mowers mingle with the buzzing of the frenetic bumble bee as it works from one fragrant bloom to another. Summer; a time for idly watching the dancing dragonflies in their mating ritual, their jewelled colours flashing red, blue and green in warm dappled sunlight, reflecting on the still water of the garden pond.

An English garden in all its summer splendour is a haven for felines. The borders provide shade as does the bay tree and the shed. The lawn is a place to sprawl and be admired.

With summer comes the outdoors, garden furniture and gatherings, the smells of outdoor cooking – and the odd piece of stolen chicken may be had. During the hot afternoons, cats will find shady cool spots to pass the listless hours.

It is the early evening when crepuscular creatures gather. This is a time to watch what other cats are up to, a time to ensure that the territory remains unsullied by invaders. And, sometimes, a time for Thutmose to come along and see how his daughters are growing up.

Then there are the bugs. Bugs that buzz about in the warm evening air, dancing hither and thither, just begging to be chased and caught. Bugs make interesting things to chase – and there's good eating to be had on a bug once it's been caught. A bit crunchy sometimes, but tasty, nonetheless.

A clowder of cats

Warm summer breeze
Soft rustling of the leaves
Azure skies with vapour trails
Linking the high fluffy clouds
***

Languid summer days
Heady scents on summer haze
Crepuscular feline gatherings
On balmy summer evenings
***

Basking indolent hours
Among fragrant flowers
These are our seasons in the sun
They'll be gone 'ere they're barely begun
***

Tortoises

The humans have four tortoises. They are strange things, really and of little interest to cats. We check under the bonnet to see if the motor is still going from time to time, but otherwise, we pay little attention but they provide little in the way of fun for us – apart, that is, from Berenike who seems to find their activities fascinating. Easily pleased, that's what I say.

Jess

One evening in May, they were left outside accidentally over night. The following morning, Jess was missing. As there had been badgers digging around, it was presumed that he had been taken and eaten. Badgers can do this apparently. Worried about what might have happened to him, they put notices in neighbours' doors asking for any news if he was seen – or, worse, evidence that he had been eaten.

Two days later, a neighbour brought him back, having discovered him stomping across their lawn. Everyone here was relieved – which means life will be a little easier again…

Jess, on the other hand carries on as before, none the worse for his adventure:

Oscar

Tortoises get to do a lot of sitting about and watching.

Flo

Ah, there's always good eating on a bit of cactus… now, how do you get started?

Moe

There's good eating on a piece of sun-dried clover.

Sophie, My Mother

My mother's human goes off to the United States every so often. So instead of leaving Sophie to her own devices in an empty house, she is temporarily re-homed with us for the duration. Is she grateful for this? Is she doggies do dos! She immediately takes up residence on the fridge and sets about terrorising the host cats. From this vantage point she can observe all comings and goings through the catflap. Any cat that dares to poke a head through it gets treated to a right royal hiss. The kittens didn't know which day of the week it was - they aren't used to being hissed at by anyone other than Cleo, well, Cleo and their own mother… well, Cleo, their mother, me, Bast, Isis and Hat, so this came as a rude shock.

And anyone who thinks that Thutmose is a miserable, cantankerous, hissy ingrate hasn't met my mother. She even hissed at ME! Yes, ME! I'm speechless. ME!

Felix Domesticus, Calculating Cat

Tabby tiger, jellicle, ginger or calico;
Our green eyes follow you wherever you go.
From the bedroom window, and the kitchen door;
We know where you've been, where you're going, where you're at;
Felix domesticus; the watchful cat.

***

Inscrutable and devious we sleep in the sun;
We don't really doze, ever ready to leap and run;
From the garden gate, the drive and the stair;
We know what you're doing, what you're thinking, where you're at;
Felix domesticus; the wily cat.

***

Fastidious and attentive, we always take note;
Feigning indolence as we groom our tabby coat.
From the hall and attic, the narrow alleyway;
We know who you are, who you've seen, what you're at;
Felix domesticus; the omniscient cat.

***

Apparently indifferent, we see all around;
We'll pad along behind you with barely a sound;
From high in a tree, or across the road;
We know where you were, your plans today, what you're at;
Felix domesticus; the inscrutable cat.

***

Green eyes, yellow eyes, golden and blue;
Eyes of every shade, hiding and watching you.
From the comfort of the duvet, the cold of the great outdoors;
We keep tabs on where you go, who you see, what you're at;
Felix domesticus, the calculating cat.

***

www.ingramcontent.com/pod-product-compliance
Lightning Source LLC
Chambersburg PA
CBHW041429090426
42744CB00002B/11